A Division of G/L Publications   Glendale, California, U.S.A.

More Than A Spectator

by HAROLD F. LEESTMA

COVER DESIGN BY RICHARD SPURLIN
COVER PHOTO BY DANA BODNAR
INSIDE PHOTOS BY
BYRON BUCK
MIKE ELLIOT
STEVE BROWNING
DOUGLAS GILBERT
HAROLD M. LAMBERT STUDIOS, INC.
H. ARMSTRONG ROBERTS

Published by
Regal Books Division, G/L Publications
Glendale, California 91209, U.S.A.

Library of Congress Catalog Card No. 74-82676
ISBN 0-8307-0302-0

4037

To the members of Lake Hills Community Church,
who are meeting the times with active,
enthusiastic faith—
as *participants*, not merely as *spectators*.

More Than A Spectator

A commitment
is more than just
an admiration.

It means I have to offer my life
in deep involvement
in Christ's life.
In His teachings,
in His moral standards,
in His death and resurrection.
In everything He's said and done.

It means I have to share
in deep involvement
in lives of people—
not standing by as a

watching to see how it goes,
but to be there
where it's happening.

A Place

Every man needs this.

A place to stand.
A Place
that's solid and secure.
A center of certainty.
A place that you know will
not give way
no matter what floods come.
A place to stand.

And then, a place to fill.
A sense of meaning,
of purpose,
of usefulness.
A Place
that you believe is yours,
where you are,
to serve your God
and your fellowman.
A Place
to stand—and
a place to fill.

DIFFICULTIES

Some people
see the

DIFFICULTIES

of believing
so keenly
that they never become
Christians.

And some
who are Christians
see the

DIFFICULTIES

of not believing
so keenly
that they have no sympathy
for those who do not
believe.

I Went to God

I went to God
having done my very best,
but far from perfect
and not really ready
at all.

And the Good News was
that He loved me!
He didn't condemn me
or turn me down.
He knew me.
Knew what I was intent
on achieving
but could not.

And I suppose if I had listened
closely,
I might have heard Him say,
"Well!
I am a bit surprised.
But I love you just the same."

Ever since then
He's been helping me to get ready.
Remaking me
in His image.

Not Some Little Storehouse

God is unlimited.
He is beyond my comprehension.
Not out of reach—
I didn't say that.
But all about Him
is not comprehended.

I can see only the present.
I've tried to see
around the next corner
but I can't.

He can.

He's an unlimited God
who isn't limited by corners.
He sees and knows
and get things ready.
Then when I turn the corner
it's all set—
all His infinite resources!

Not Some Little Storehouse

of my own.

shatterproof

He found a new life,
a new direction.
And now he is solid
and certain
that he stands
within an
unbreakable
love.

A love that
all through those
wasted years
never really left him,
but kept touching him,
nudging him,
pulling and tugging—
until at last
he understands
this love that cannot be broken.

Your History and Mine

God has an unwavering plan.
All the intricacies
and complexities
of life
aren't going to upset it
or spoil it.

He's moving through history
today—
everywhere.
God is at work.

He's moving in the history
of your life
and mine
with an unwavering,
unswerving
purpose.

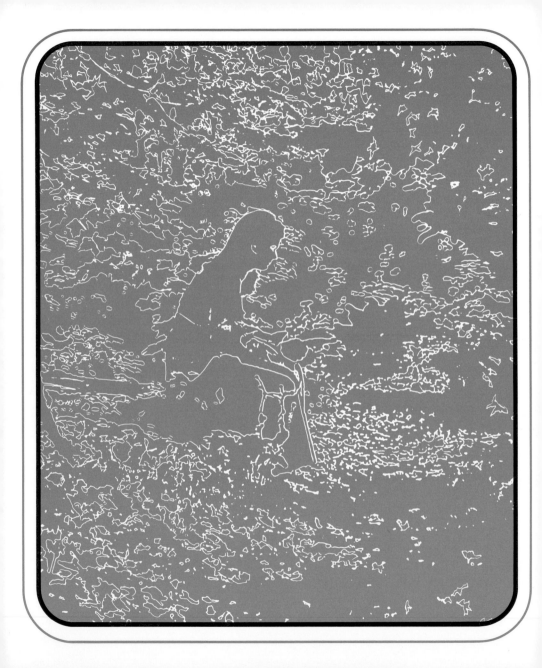

Light

God is

Light

In Him is no darkness
at all.
Nothing puts out that

Light

We may not see Him
as clearly as we would like.
The light may seem dim at times.
Or perhaps He doesn't yet shed

Light

on the thing we want immediately.

Is that some fault of His?

New Motorcycle

It takes coordination.
A few new things to learn—
a little hard to get started.

You take the first turn.
You waver a little.
You learn to balance.
At first it's a bit hard
to keep going.

But it's harder
to stop.
Through the woods,
out among the pines,
nobody there.

You circle around,
wind blowing in your face.
You don't want to stop.

That's the Christian life, too.
Not easy to get started.
Then—hard to keep going.

But when you've experienced
God's love,
you don't want to stop.

You want to keep going—
with the wind of His Spirit
blowing across your soul.

Is He Serious

Is it possible
to be a Christian?
If not—what's the use
of trying?

Did Jesus really intend
that we put into practice
what He taught?

Or did He intend
merely to inspire us—
like poetry,
a beautiful piece of art,
or some great music?
Something to be looked at
and admired
but certainly
not to be taken
seriously?

Why, He even said
you have
to be perfect
as your heavenly Father
is perfect!
What do we do about that?

Here are these sayings
of Christ.
On the surface
at times
they don't seem to fit
this twentieth century.
They look impractical.

And we'd rather have it
all wrapped up,
neatly packaged,
with rules,
instructions,
by-laws,
minute details.

Instead, we're given
strong principles,
told to be empowered
with the Holy Spirit,
and then
to work it out for ourselves
with Him!

He Is Serious

BUT—
doesn't Jesus know about me?
Indeed—He does.

He knows about your misery
and your grandeur.
He knows about your degradation
and about your potential.
He knows about your sin.
But He also knows about your
salvation.

Jesus looked into the faces
of men
who were ambitious,
hot-tempered,
unstable and
doubting.
And He believed they were capable
of developing into spiritual giants.

He looks right at you.
And He says,
"You can do it."

Possibilities

I suppose
a struggling artist
could throw down his brush
and stamp his foot
and say,
*"This kind of picture
just can't be painted!"*

Then let him step into
an art gallery.
He'll see with his own eyes
how the great masters
have painted.

The Devil's Nickname

IF we gave the devil
a nickname,
it might be

"So-so."

After all,
his business
is mediocrity—
trying to get
the standard
down.
He tries to get us
to turn out
an ordinary performance.

He likes the words
second-rate,
average,
just getting by,

Maximum Performance

If life is only
just getting by,
it's not the life
Christ asked me to live.

Being satisfied
with little results
is less than my best.
Second-rate.
Below par.
The world may settle for a
minimum performance
but God asks for the

Maximum

No trivialities—
not when I'm working
for my Lord!

You see,
He has been
so extravagant
Himself.
He was extravagant
in His love.
And in His life.

He didn't send
an announcement
from heaven.
He sent Himself.

He didn't merely do
some good deeds.
He stretched Himself
on a cross
and died for me.

LIFTED

His life seemed
something like that old war sub.
Barnacles, rust
and decay.
At the bottom,
broken.

It was

LIFTED

and towed into drydock,
repaired, remolded,
renamed,
and recommissioned.
Then sent out again
on course.

It happened to this
man too,
and he went into daring
heroic service
for our Lord.

Toward the Mark

You're not going to make it
on your own, you know.

Did you expect
to achieve it
in your own strength?
But that plodding,
vain struggle
will disappear
in your surrender
to God—
knowing He loves you,
forgives you,
saves you,
enables you.

With this power of Christ
all things are possible.
And that despairing cry,
"I have to . . ."
"I ought . . ."
is changed to a glorious shout:
"I can, Lord!
I will!"

The Follower

He became a follower of Jesus
and found it difficult.
He had weaknesses
and hesitations.
Times when he didn't
run fast enough.
Then there were
impetuous, ambitious moments.
Times when he ran too fast.

But after he had seen
the resurrected Christ,
at last his life was
synchronized.

They put him in prison,
took him through the big gates,
behind the thick walls,
down the narrow corridor
to the inner dungeon.
Chained him
hand and foot.

And what did this
once-hesitant,
once-impetuous man
do now?

Completely trusting Christ,
Peter slept—
and woke
tuned to divine timing.

No more chains!

THE BOTTOM RUNG

That's where it happens.
Right there
at the bottom of the ladder.
That's where God meets us—
in the eternal now
where we are.

He doesn't come to us
in our rightness
but in our wrongness.
Not in our strength
but in our weakness.
Not in our goodness
but in our sin
and loneliness.

That's where conversion
takes place.
That's when the new life begins.
On the bottom rung
of the ladder
when God meets us
in our helplessness
and our hopelessness
and we say to Him,
"I need You!"

Awareness

Ptolemy counted the stars
1,800 years ago
and said there were 1,022.
Galileo with his telescope
later counted 5,000.
In 1900 the estimate was 300 billion.
Then it was doubled
and trebled
and men spoke of galaxies
and island universes.
Today it's metagalaxies—
galaxies of galaxies—
on into unimaginable

Infinity

Which brings us to God,
who is my Father.
That is His bigness, His power.
That's my Father—
my Father who cares.

The Word

He has freed me,
given me a New Life.
Forgiven me!
Forever.

In that word—forgiven—
is the biggest thing
that ever happened to me.
This word
is real
and very personal.
It's mine.
And because of it I am freed
to say with Jesus—
and freed to act upon it—
"Father, forgive them."

Faith-sharing

If faith is to be shared
it must be real.
And if it is real
it will be shared:

"I believe in God,
the Father almighty,
maker of heaven and earth."
And He's my Father.
yours, too!

I believe in Jesus Christ,
His only Son, our Lord."
And He's my Lord!
yours, too?

Live Wire

Notice the quarterback
right up there behind the lines
calling the signals,
grabbing the ball, running back,
being attacked
by some pretty big men,
finding a way to throw that pass
to his receiver
for a touchdown.
He's at ease
in the midst of conflict.

The basketball star
moves down the floor,
two or three tall men
blocking his way.
He shoots that ball
and it goes—right through the hoop.
That's inner calm under tension.

Jesus didn't say, "Come to me,
all you who are loafing,
who never get involved!"
He promised rest in the struggle—
not from it.
I think one continuous nap
would be pretty monotonous.

Reality

Jesus refused to panic.

There they were
in a storm. At sea.
Around Him, His disciples—
hardened fishermen—cried,
"We shall all be lost!"

"Peace. Peace.
Be still,"
said our Lord.
And the winds and the waves
died down.

Yes, look at the storm.
It's real.
You can feel the wind
and you know the unsteadiness
of the ship you're in.

But Christ is real, too.
Look, Peter, James,
John!
He's there in the ship
with you!

Did you forget?

There's Enough

"Thank You, God,
for something of which

There's Enough

He has enough love
to cover
all your past.
He has enough power
and wisdom
to help you meet every
present situation.
And He has enough light
to brighten your future
forever.

Live by that!
Live by His love
and His promise.

For all your days

There's Enough

SPEAKING OF HEIGHTS

God has built a mountain in my life;
an accumulation of
experience after experience,
built up
through the years:
His forgiving, merciful love.
His careful guidance.
His marvelous, exact timing of things.
His provision for my need.
His affection and friendship.

By faith,
I live on the top of the mountain.

Matching
the Times

This Christian faith
is relevant,
real,
and rich.
It's ready to rise
to the occasion.

Confusion?
Crisis?
Conflict?
This faith can
match the times.

Demanding—yes.
But it's durable,
dynamic,
delightful—
and it works
under pressure.

It's workable at all times—
facing life
or death.
For nothing can separate us
from God's love
in Christ.

For today,
everything you need.
And some day
at the end of the road
you can say,
"So long—
I'll be seeing you!"

May God help you
live by this faith
and die by it too.
It matches the times.

Participants

You're moving on the way
God has planned for you
toward the goal:
"Be perfect!"

He gives His blessings,
and at times withholds them,
as your life
grows more Christlike
day by day.
You are walking in a place
of high privilege,
right now.

And some day at the end
do you picture yourself standing
on a high hill
gazing up at the Celestial City,
and saying,
"It's so bright and beautiful
it reflects way down here
on me!"

No, you won't be looking
at that light.
You're going to be in that light.

You'll not be a spectator
of a glorious eternity.
You're going to be a

Participant

You're moving on the way